I MADE THESE MISTAKES ON ETSY SO YOU WON'T HAVE TO

Keela Butler

Copyright © 2022 Keela Butler
All rights reserved.
ISBN: 9798367606492

DEDICATION

To the next group of thinkers, leaders, dreamers, creatives and go getters. The entrepreneurs of the world.

CONTENTS

	Dedication	i
1	Be Ordinary	1
2	Do It All	5
3	Violate Trademarks	10
4	Zero Marketing	15
5	Devalue Connections	20
6	Avoid Custom Orders	25
7	Ignore Expenses	30
8	Short-Sighted	36
9	Bad Mockups	41
10	Take A Break	45

BE ORDINARY

A common pitfall many Etsy sellers fall into is seeking to blend in rather than stand out. There are many success stories of people making hundreds of thousands of revenue in sales during their first year or less so we automatically think, ok this is my blueprint. Sales is not a one size fit all model. What worked for someone else may not necessarily work for you. There is this big debate about creating a general store versus a specific niche store. Many have found success in the general store model which means although they may focus on one type of product, they offer several categories.

When I first started out I wasn't sure what to sell. My first sale was actually election related due to the timing and shortly after that I started offering all types of other categories. I had a category for election merchandise, Valentine's Day, positive quotes, you name it and I had it. I never actually took the time to plan a business model or business plan, let alone do any real research. On top of that,

I forgot about selling products I would even consider wearing. Everything was about making a dollar and since I was new to the platform, I went the trial and error route. Wasted a lot of valuable time when I could have been creating a brand and defining my target customer.

Exploring various niches is not a horrible idea however many are completely oversaturated. If you don't believe me just type in a few popular keywords and look at the thousands of options available. For example, major holidays are huge on Etsy. Everyone wants to provide an ugly Christmas sweater or teacher mug for the holidays because it is a hot quarter for shopping. However, you don't have to sell a Christmas themed item during the Christmas season just to get a sale.

You may already have a really great product that sells well but you want to position it as more of a gift. Maybe you update your keywords or even adjust your product photo to promote it as a great present for mom or a friend. You're not obligated to jump on every niche because it appears to be working for everyone else. Another example for me is Halloween. Its a billion dollar industry and the favorite holiday of many. I thought I did everything right by checking all the trends, selecting great mockups, and posting my listings long before the Halloween season to get a jumpstart. Smart right? I did not make one sale. The reasons why potentially are endless but the point is I had a lot of other choices I could have made instead of jumping into an already saturated niche. Maybe I should have taken a best-selling product I already possessed and adjusted the colors for the season. Or perhaps I could have showcased my products with fall colors as the primary photo during that time. Better yet, I could have skipped the holiday completely and focused my time on researching keywords, reviewing my stats, and updating my social media. I wasn't obligated to jump on the popular train and neither are you. If you research many of those sellers in the forefront of these best-selling products for the most popular keywords, you will often find that it isn't a new listing or even design. They've been at it for a while.

When it comes to design, Etsy is very trend oriented. You will easily know what the trends are because you'll see them over and over again. Now there is a difference between following a trend and just copying someone's design. Many of us have done it and I can honestly say I have had some success. More often than not however I've had a lot of unsold products and thankfully not any infringement reports from the original seller. We'll come back to that topic later. I consider myself to be a business person. I even have a degree to prove it. But there has to be an element of creativity involved if you want a large amount of sales. When you take someone else's design, even if you do bother to adjust a couple of tiny elements, you're basically saying that you aren't creative.

Not only are you not creative but you're not willing to take any risks. Instead of just swiping what you think is a design that is selling well for yourself, take it to the next level. Go through that sellers' reviews. Look at what sizes or colors they offer and what they could be offering. Improve upon what has already been done and aim to be number one. Don't just settle for a few one off sales because you decided to charge a couple of dollars less and you're hoping someone randomly chooses your product instead. Elevate the design, mockup, offering, everything. Better yet, come up with something original. You can research trends without having to produce a design or product exactly like everyone else. Some of the most up-and-coming shops don't follow trends at all. Maybe your focus is on quality or customer service. Once again, find what makes you stand out and don't be afraid to take risks.

DO IT ALL

Becoming a one woman show originally started off as a badge of honor for me but as time progressed, I quickly learned that I needed help. You don't have to do it all. Quite frankly you shouldn't do it all. Everyone has strengths and weaknesses. The sooner you identify what they are, the sooner you can improve upon your skillset and get your hands on the right resources. Design was a huge motivator for me getting on Etsy in the first place. I had a love for graphic design although I was a bit of an amateur and wanted to do it all. I actually did pretty well when it came to more of the basic designs such as a lot of quotes and overall typography. When I decided I wanted more graphics and color, I began to teach myself more design techniques. I even spent a lot of money on this high powered software and watched countless videos. My skillset did improve however I was taking hours upon hours sometimes even days to get a more polished look if I ever even accomplished it.

I also found myself having to compromise my vision and settle for a design I was more capable of producing. One day I started to wonder how on earth anyone else was doing this. When did they find the time to create all of these amazing designs and put them on 500 products plus in one store? Then one day I started to notice many shops had the exact same design and I finally understood my dilemma. All of these sellers had help! They were not doing it all alone like I was. I discovered numerous amazing artists on Etsy and a lot of other great online platforms in addition that offered fantastic, professional graphics for a small cost. I could now devote more of my time into mocking up the product for display, exploring keywords, and many other tasks that were more of my strengths. There are also a lot of free or subscription based websites that have unlimited quantities of artwork you can manipulate and make your own without having to worry about stealing anyone else's work.

It's very important to seek outside counsel and wisdom as you build your business. More than likely you're not the first person to do what you're doing and there's someone or maybe even a group that has gone before you, hence this book. In the beginning I did a lot of looking around but didn't exactly take a step back to really understand the process behind being a best seller and study what could work. I didn't truly find a mentor that was doing exactly what I was doing and had achieved a level of success I desired until after a year in. A huge part of that was because of all of the mistakes I had made and although some would still say I was successful, I found myself having to start over.

We have access to so many other amazing entrepreneurs that can offer a lot of knowledge and save you a world of mistakes. I actually found my mentor on YouTube. I started off with a great couple that a friend referred me to but I didn't take their advice as seriously as I should have. They actually interviewed my now mentor on their channel one day and I was so intrigued by her number of sales and the time she was able accomplish it in. I really saw myself in her and thought, if she can do it then so can I. I started off just watching her videos on YouTube which I thought were absolutely incredible. I couldn't believe someone would give away all of this great advice for absolutely free. After watching her for a few of weeks I noticed she offered to review other Etsy seller shops for a fee. I jumped at the chance to hear from her. I thought to myself, I've been at this for a while now. Over 1 year at that point. If someone wants to give me a shortcut and critique my shop then I'm all about it! Constructive criticism didn't scare me at all. I wanted her to be brutally honest with me and although she wasn't brutal, she was definitely honest. So many mistakes pointed out in a matter of 45 minutes. I can only imagine where my store could have been had I reached out to someone like her sooner.

Never be afraid to pay for knowledge. It's truly an investment and more often than not, you get what you pay for. There's a saying that only fools despise wisdom and instruction. If you're looking to accelerate your sales, mentorship and counsel is a great tool. You may be reading this and already have a team assembled, but are you using them to their fullest potential? A great leader knows how to delegate and get the most out of their resources. For example, if you're selling hand crafted ceramic mugs and you know during the holiday season business always skyrockets, why haven't you pivoted yet for those months? I understand you want to maintain product quality but you're not the only person that can paint a mug.

Hire local help or even a print on demand company to help print orders so you're not missing out on sales and delaying orders. Can a problem occur if someone steps in? Absolutely! Once you get to a certain number of sales, expect it. But I assure you, Jeff Bezos is not over at Amazon packaging boxes. Maybe you even have an employee who answers customer questions or helps ship out packages. Your spouse or sibling might be your very own personal assistant on occasion.

Regardless of who it is, find a task you can trust them to do. I know of sellers that wanted a personal touch to their clothes so they started sewing in their own personal tags and personalizing their packaging. They never even took the time to see if the manufacturer they were working with would do it even for an added fee, and guess what? They did. How many more sales could they have achieved if they weren't busy taking on responsibilities that could have been assigned elsewhere. You have to loosen the reins sometimes and outsource help. That's truly how you expand and scale your business in the long run so consider yourself ahead of the curve.

VIOLATE TRADEMARKS

Violating trademarks almost shut down my entire business for good. Can you imagine the time and effort you put into your Etsy shop all going down the drain? Well it almost happened to me. I was completely clueless of Etsy's policies when it came to trademark infringement. I'm not even sure I knew a policy existed at the time. I had been selling for about 7-8 months at that time and was barely at 100 sales. To say I felt disappointed would have been an understatement. During that time I took a random trip to Chicago which has become one of my favorite cities and attended a NBA game for the very first time. What an exhilarating experience! The fandemonium as I like to call it was just out of this world.

If you know anything about Chicago then you know the legacy of the Chicago Bulls. Many had counted this team out but they were slowly building their way back up and the game was just sensational! I looked out into the crowd and saw nothing but a sea of red and black everywhere. When in Rome, do as the Romans so I was decked out in my newly bought Chicago gear. You would think the selection process for gear would have been easy but I was so shocked at some of the prices for these items. $30 for a plain Chicago t-shirt? It had to have been below 50 degrees that night. No one even saw it! But like the other fans I had to have my gear so I bought it anyway along with a hat and a few other things to look like I belong.

When I came back home I had this bright idea that I would get into the sports niche and make a killing! And boy did I. My sales went completely through the roof! It was like nothing I had seen before up to that point. I went from trying to reach 100 sales for the year to expecting a thousand in a matter of two months! My third party printer originally gave me a hard time with the full team names but I soon found my way around it and as fast as they could print these items, I was selling them. No advertising, no fancy mock ups, women and men of all ages became my customers. I thought to myself this is just too good to be true. Why aren't more people doing this? Have I truly just outsmarted everyone?

Well turns I hadn't. It was actually quite the opposite. As my popularity began to rise, so did the target on my shop. Slowly representatives from these different sports leagues started to report my shop. In my mind I thought, I'm untouchable! A few tweaks here and there and I'll be just fine. Big deal if they take down one listing because I had hundreds more. I couldn't lose. Unfortunately I found out I actually could lose and lose big! Etsy Legal sent me an email giving me a final warning and that's when I knew, it was over. I had to painstakingly take down every one of my listings that even remotely could violate a trademark.

Not only had I printed trademarks on my products but even the way I promoted the items were infringement. I had no clue I couldn't put certain words in my title or keyword tags but that's because I didn't do my homework. I never took the time to read the seller handbook or any other documentation available. After all this is Etsy's platform. They make up the rules and the least I could do was read them. During the first few email warnings, I still never took the time to fully read their policies so I had no real understanding of everything I was doing wrong. Surprisingly I'm actually an avid reader and had I taken the twenty minutes or so to read the handbook, I may have actually turned a bad idea into a good one without infringing upon anyone else's rights or feeling forced to take every listing down but I was just terrified at that point.

The United States Patent and Trademark Office provide a trademark database that can be electronically searched in a matter of seconds and save you a world of trouble down the road. You really should be using this database before you list any products on Etsy. You would be surprised at popular quotes or even smiley face emojis that have been trademarked in the past. It also doesn't hurt to check back every now and then and make sure you're not violating anyone's registered trademark. If you ever decide you want to register your own trademark, you can apply on this same website and they'll walk you through the process.

The database will also show you pending applications. It's important you get a full understanding of the database and how to interpret your search results before you start searching. There are several search options including basic word mark search, design search, and multiple search fields to utilize for a full and thorough search. If your particular phrase for example shows up in the search results as a live trademark, you'll want to go back to the drawing board. It's up to you if you want to modify what you have but be sure to research that as well. When in doubt, just don't use it. Etsy isn't readily available to answer these type of questions which is why they provide a policy so you really have to use your best judgement and play it safe.

Do not be fooled by what other sellers are doing. You can find trademark infringement all over Etsy but do not, I repeat do not take the bait! It's not worth it. You might find ten Etsy shops selling Disney products left and right and you just so happen to be the unlucky one that gets reported. You can't trust what you see other people selling especially if they haven't been doing it very long. The same exact scenario happened to me. After a few weeks of selling sports trademarked products I noticed other sellers starting to do the same. They wanted in on the sales but had no clue what they were really in for. Months later after the entire incident I looked back and couldn't find those same products being sold anywhere on Etsy. I even had a hard time finding many of the sellers so don't depend on the competition to know the rules for you. Use the resources we talked about prior and avoid receiving a violation at all costs.

    I won't tell you how many warnings I received before the final warning because it all truly does vary. I've heard of sellers receiving a handful of warnings first and I've heard of others maybe receiving one before losing their entire shop which also includes your ability to every buy on Etsy again. This is where originality really has its rewards because you're less likely to violate anyone's rights when you're relying on your own creativity. One final note. If something seems too good to be true, it probably is. Think to yourself why an obvious design or saying may not be found anywhere on Etsy and use the tools we discussed.

ZERO MARKETING

Marketing can seem like a daunting task to many but let's breakdown simply what it is. Marketing is the process of getting people interested in your products or service. If you're not willing to market your business then you have to ask yourself is this a real business for you or just a hobby. Marketing isn't reserved for only giant corporations either. It can be as simple as a flyer or even posting a photo on Facebook. Etsy offers several opportunities to market your shop and they're connected to various other platforms which can be effective as well.

    Truthfully there are a lot of mixed reviews for Etsy advertisements however when you're just starting out, they can make a huge difference. One of the advantages of Etsy is the fact that it's a marketplace. Hundreds of millions of customers visit the platform daily actively looking to buy. When you advertise on Etsy, you're putting your product or service in front of millions of people who not only have the potential buying power but the willingness and motivation to buy. Over 95% of my customers on Etsy have always been strangers but it didn't matter. I was supplying what they were in demand of and the beautiful part of it is, more often than not you don't have to have this longstanding reputation.

Etsy ads can move you to the front of the line in front of even best sellers when you budget accordingly. Starting out I didn't really utilize Etsy ads because I wasn't seeing results fast enough but without the ads it can take a few weeks before customers begin to find you within the algorithm. If you pay attention to what's drawing people in to click on your ad or buy, you now have the knowledge to improve your listing. There is an option that allows you to review what Etsy has considered relevant keywords within your ad and it allows you to further target the right audience. It's so easy to implement and no extra design work is needed but be sure you're monitoring your progress so you can focus on the listings that are showing results. Typically you want to get a sale first before you advertise the listing to boost your way to best seller and get a better return on your investment.

Avoiding social media for marketing is definitely a huge mistake. I was totally against creating a social media presence in the beginning because it sounded like so much work. Where was I going to find time to update a social media page on multiple platforms in addition to everything else I had to do? And like I just mentioned, I figured the best advertising was on Etsy. How can I trust someone browsing Facebook was going to all of a sudden want to buy what I was selling as they look through their friends photos? Where was the guarantee in that? Truth is, there wasn't one.

It can be a challenge to predict who will actually take action if you put your product or service in front of them. How many ads do we ignore daily wanting our money and attention? Social media however is not just about sales. It forces you to build a brand and cultivate an audience for your business. There are millions of people signed up for Facebook, Instagram, Pintrest, Tik Tok and more that may never come across your Etsy store in any other way but seeing your social media page. It will take work to build an online presence however if you're not willing to put the time and effort in then you're limiting yourself.

You really have to look at your business as creating value for your audience. It should be your mission to reach as many people as you can because in your mind you have something of value that they should want. Are there successful shops without a social media presence? Absolutely. But just think about how many more sales they could have if the extra effort was put in to simply update their

Instagram or Pinterest every time they had a sale or new product.

    The process really can't get much easier when it comes to posting unless you hired someone else to do it which you always could. There is a lot of great technology and apps available to help you come up with content, tags, and even schedule all of your posts. Several platforms even allow the customer to buy directly from the social media page without ever seeing an Etsy website. Social media appears to be here to stay so it would be wise to use it to your benefit and spread the word about what you're working on.

    Google advertising is one of the best forms of marketing you should be using and not just because Google is considered king when it comes to search engine technology. Many would consider it to be the most powerful company in the world. Over 4 billion people use Google so it doesn't take a rocket scientist to know, there is an unlimited audience viewing a Google related page daily. Etsy already incorporates Google advertising into marketing your shop whether you know it or not but you can take it a step further.

    Once you know your audience and how you want to target them, you can setup a very effective Google ad and bring in new customers. I made the mistake of only dabbling with Google ads but had I been fully committed to building my brand and learning more about my audience, I could have experienced more success. It's easy to blow through money with Google ads because the traffic is so high pretty much all of the time. This is why you need a strategy before you get started. If you just jump out there, you're going to find yourself quickly out of money and questioning why you thought this was a good idea. Believe me, you can make it work for you. Google brings in billions of dollars in search ads alone each year.

DEVALUE CONNECTIONS

A lot of times when someone starts out on a new business venture, they turn to those closest to them first for business. They go to their family, friends, church, sorority, and anyone else who knows them. You might even offer them a discount because you're just hoping they'll buy something and best case scenario, like it enough to tell someone else. Not me. My very first customer on Etsy was a total stranger. I was beyond excited and had the reassurance that I could do this! My confidence went through the roof. A person I had never met in my life that knew nothing about me or my business made a purchase. I had zero sales or reviews at the time. I thought to myself if I can sell to one stranger then surely I can sell to another and another. Friends and family, who needs them?

I wanted to prove that I could build a following strictly based on the product itself and without some boost from those I know. What I was actually doing at the time was robbing myself of a jumpstart. I eventually did gain friends and family as customers but had I went to them first, perhaps I would have already had several sales to show. And then maybe I would have had a few five star reviews as well. I received all of those things later but the point is, I could have started off that way and possibly a listing that sold once may have sold ten times. Never underestimate the power of a great review and that includes word of mouth promotion.

How many times have you visited a new restaurant or saw the latest movie because someone told you how great it was? Now I want you to think of how many times you looked up the reviews to see what others had to say. I can honestly say there aren't many new restaurants I have tried where someone somewhere didn't vouch for it first. I could say the same about so many other services or product lines. Use your connections and give them the best experience possible.

One of the benefits of utilizing your everyday connections is the feedback you can receive. If you have friends or family members, maybe even co-workers that you consider your target audience then ask for their thoughts. Take a poll of their interests in relation to what you offer and ask for constructive criticism on what you currently sell or plan to in the future. People actually pay good money for this type of feedback and you can receive it for free. My mistake was always wanting to research the trends or look at the best sellers. Instead I should have taken more time to get to know my targeted customer.

Not every trend or best seller is going to work for your Etsy shop and customer. Another form of targeted research is viewing your audience from a different perspective. Join a Facebook group or follow an Instagram page you know would be attractive to your customer. Find out what may be considered trending for them because it may not be as obvious as you think. For example, if your audience includes a lot of teachers than you can join a community online that caters to teachers. The 100th day of school is a popular trend on Etsy. That might be a trend you want to jump on however unless you have a child in school or are a part of that community, there's a good chance you had no clue that was even a thing. Another tip is paying attention to your personal circle for that same category. If you sell jewelry then start paying attention to what those around you are wearing. Ask them what made them buy that particular piece. What do they like about it? What do they wish was better? At the very least you'll know you can have them as a customer because you're creating around their advice for the best product or service possible.

As I stated earlier, I made the mistake of wanting the business of strangers more than I did of those closest to me. I really should have been volunteering my services because again, you should be creating value for someone in whatever it is you're doing. Now don't get me wrong. When I say volunteer I don't literally mean you need to give anything away unless you're comfortable doing it. That's your choice. But there's no reason why for example if you know the travel group you're apart of needs matching t-shirts and you own a t-shirt business that you would not offer your services. Or if you're in a large group setting that supports small business owners and they ask for those who own a business to come speak for a minute on what you do and how people can support you, take advantage. Why are you just sitting there? Get up and promote your business! Offer your services. Offer them value.

    I have been guilty of these mistakes more times than I can count myself. Everyone you're in any type of connection with should know what you do. Be bold! Maybe they don't need your services now but in the future that could change or someone they know may be looking for the exact thing you provide. Now you may be saying to yourself well I don't want to do a custom order or I'm too scared to work with so many people I know. What if I mess up and they're unhappy? These were my thoughts exactly. There's truly no reward without risk. Go for it and do it with the fear or apprehension. Also be prepared to hand out business cards or something tangible. Yes we're in a technology driven time but someone is more likely to revisit a piece of paper in their possession than go out of their way to look up a website in the middle of everything else that might be going on. I went so long without owning a single business card and when people would complement me on a product I made, all I would do is thank them without any mention of my store. It was a missed opportunity every single time.

AVOID CUSTOM ORDERS

Custom and personalized orders are often best sellers on Etsy. Customers want something special. Often they're looking for a gift for a loved one and want to buy them something unique. If they were looking for just the run of the mill sweater or card they would simply go to Target or some other retail store on every corner. Even knowing this I avoid custom or personalized orders for a very long time. I was determined to find the customers that were interested in what I was selling and there really is nothing wrong with that. You just will not be operating at your fullest potential. Etsy even has a search filter for personalized orders right next to free shipping and best sellers.

    Speaking of shipping, if you're concerned about the extra time and effort it will take to accommodate these orders, you should be. There are methods however of hiding additional costs such as increasing your shipping costs. What I have learned is if people want something bad enough, within reason of course they will pay the cost. Think about if you were shopping for yourself or a gift for someone else. Are you really going to shop on Etsy just to choose a beautiful but typical greeting card you can find in Dollar Tree or are you going to choose the one that has a custom hand drawing of your friend and dog for her birthday? If you create a template and overall game plan for custom orders, it can be a lot easier than you think.

    Say for example you want to sell matching holiday pajamas with matching t-shirts. Instead of leaving the t-shirt completely blank and open for any type of message, you create a design that reads the current year and family last name. On Etsy you would select the personalization option and allow for the buyer to enter solely their family name. Depending on your process the entry may be automated or you may have to manually update the design. If the latter than you could have a ready-made template where you can simply just pop in the name and submit for printing. In this scenario you're looking at multiple sales in one order so you're already paying yourself for the extra time needed to customize this order. Matching group products with personalization are huge sellers on Etsy. Imagine a grandmother that can buy all of her grandchildren the same quality gift but with their names and birthdate. Or a wedding party that is looking to buy each bridesmaid a custom tote or robe with the name or nickname of each person.

    Earlier we talked about the power of your connections but you can't be afraid to establish new connections. Especially for business. Networking is key to obtaining more orders, especially larger orders. There are numerous groups, organizations, and more who are always in need of a customized product on a large scale. I recently went on a cruise and happen to sit at a table of vey accomplished women. I talked more in depth to one about my Etsy store and she was shocked that I hadn't told more people about my business. T-shirts have been one of my best sellers and she reminded me there were hundreds of people just in our group alone that could use my services for the annual t-shirt design. She herself is a member of other organizations and they're always looking to create a new t-shirt every single year. When she asked if I did custom orders, I really didn't know what to say because I was too embarrassed to tell her no.

    Every person you meet is a potential networking opportunity. You could easily receive the bulk of your business from custom orders. Once you deliver and develop a good reputation, many of the same organizations will need you again. Many of us have attended family reunions where there's a different t-shirt every single year for the same group of people and sometimes not any further personalization but literally the same design for each shirt. There's also the opportunity to upsell and make available other products with a similar design such as a party favor or perhaps you received so many orders you just want to throw in something additional. Never underestimate the power of adding a small personalization to any product or service you may sell.

A bonus I want to add to this chapter is spending more time discussing group orders. More often than not if you are selling a group of products together, each product differs so you can still consider it to be more of a special order. If you're not selling any type of group or bundle of products, you need to get on that immediately. Don't take for granted someone will see that you have multiple designs of the same product and just order more. Think for the customer. Create that group listing and make it super appealing. Show them why it is they need 3 planners instead of one. Use persuasive language in your title and description like matching, group, and custom. Brainstorm upcoming events or days that may warrant an assembly of people. Is it gift giving season and you want to help your customer provide a gift for multiple people? Is there an upcoming gathering where multiple people would want to be identified as being together? Maybe your customer is the lead on a certain project and is responsible for providing this product to several people but has specific requests. We can all think of a group listing that would make sense. Invest the effort upfront and once it takes off, you'll be glad you did.

IGNORE EXPENSES

Forget about sales for a moment. Do you have any clue how much money you're spending? Are you counting the costs for running your business? If I asked you what is Etsy charging you per sale and what are their fees, could you even answer? If you don't know the answer to that last question, go find out then come back and continue reading. Do your research. These are questions you should not only answer but have answered before you opened your Etsy shop and ask yourself on an ongoing basis. Look at the world we're living in. Costs and prices are constantly changing. Even Etsy has made changes over the years and if you're not paying attention, you could find yourself lining someone else's pockets instead of your own.

You need to know what Etsy is charging you. Are you paying for Etsy Plus or just using basic Etsy? Etsy has a number of fees including listing, private listing, renewal, shipping label, transaction, VAT, pattern, advertising, payment, and deposit fees. Let's also not forget taxes. I had owned a store for well over a year and one day a friend asked me what were the fees to sell on Etsy and surprisingly to myself, I could not answer. I had gotten so caught up in designing and sales numbers that I stopped looking at each individual fee. You may say to yourself, well I know what my overall profit is but that isn't enough. You should be able to account for every dollar and cent Etsy is charging you and understand why. Luckily there are great resources such as Etsy's payment and invoice details as well as the Etsy fee calculator which you can google however, you want to confirm that it's updated. I remember when my sales started to pick up and I was thrilled however every time I would look at my bank account it seemed as if I was losing money. I could not seem to keep balance between costs and income.

    Finally I started to wonder, well when is Etsy paying me what's owed? I was so use to barely making any sales, when things began to pick up I didn't even know my own payment schedule. I was paying my third party supplier the costs of the orders immediately however Etsy was only transferring my revenue every two weeks to my account. It was a disaster! To make matters worse, back then I didn't have a separate account for my business so I was tapping into money I had reserved for bills and other personal expenses. Read through the handbook and any other Etsy documentation you can find regarding finances and understand what you have signed up for. Stop just looking at the bottom line and actually read through your invoices. They have continued to simplify the invoice and payment screen that even a child could understand it. As a warning you may be surprised at what you find but now you will be more informed. Don't be afraid to make changes. People do it all of the time. If you need to increase your pricing or shipping then do it. Keep in mind, this is a business you're running.

Product costs are also just as important and you have to stay on top of them. With so many changes happening in the economy, the price of materials can fluctuate. It's not enough to calculate today's cost but also think about the future. If costs were to slightly go up a few cents or maybe even a dollar or more, would you still list your current price? Sure you can always adjust your prices, and I have, but you can avoid the constant adjustment if you increase your profit margin for potential increases. The mistake I would make is focusing so much on the competition that I would lower my prices to the absolute lowest for minimal profit. I didn't realize price was not the only determining factor if a customer would buy or not and instead just cheated myself out of profits. Between the Etsy fees, advertising expenses, and changing product costs, I could not keep up. I started to lose money until I learned how to set my prices based on my own calculations and perceptions instead of someone else's.

If you find yourself a great Etsy calculator or simply take the time to do the math on your own, it'll offer you a great deal of help when evaluating your product costs. Number one is just knowing what they are and confirming frequently. For a long time I only offered a lower quality product due to product costs and my other expenses at the time. As time progressed and I learned what the customer preferred, I switched solely to the higher quality version and took it a step further and found a new supplier. Don't be afraid to shop around for a new supplier even if your current company is meeting all of your other needs. Cost is crucial and will always affect the bottom line. Switching suppliers was one of the best decisions I ever made for my business.

I'll admit every blue moon I still had quality control issues as I had with the previous company and the shipping options weren't exactly varied, however I was receiving the exact same product at a lower cost. I consider that to be a win. It even allowed me to offer free shipping without increasing my overall price to what I might consider unreasonable.

Advertising expenses can truly be a worthwhile investment or an endless black hole. I relied heavily on advertising most of my first year on Etsy to get my store in front of as many people as possible specifically on Etsy and in my mind, it paid off. Customers often found me through the advertisements and I even landed several best sellers. I just knew I was racking up money so I kept the ads going and constantly reinvested profits back into my advertising budget. It took me a long time to finally realize I was not making any money. Every penny I had was being stripped away from advertising fees. It wasn't just the ads I was creating but also the offsite ads Etsy volunteered my products for. You may be thinking similar to how I was and just wanting the sales numbers plus reviews. But that was all I got.

Many of my customers were not returning and I was forced to constantly reinvest in advertising to acquire new customers. My strategy basically was only working in the short term. Perhaps if I only advertised the products I had previously sold or made modifications each week based on what was working, I could have been more cffcctivc. Etsy does an outstanding job of clearly labeling marketing fees in the invoice section to show you what is being spent and it's all in real time. Etsy ads also has an entire analytics section that show what your true return is for your ad budget and which products were ordered from being marketed. It's to consider advertising the products or services that aren't selling because they are the ones that need the extra help right? Totally wrong thought process. You always want to start with the winners.

The products that have sold based on SEO, mockup photos, and just pure interest. They will perform the best with the added advertising. If you don't have any sales yet then focus on getting a sale first and determining what you can do to make the listing more appealing or after a reasonable amount of time, re-evaluate if it's a product in demand. Don't just throw your money away. Track your spending so you can know if your current advertising strategy is meeting your set goals and if not then make some changes.

SHORT-SIGHTED

Local retail stores are a great example of planning for the upcoming seasons. When you're celebrating the 4th of July they have already stocked the back to school merchandise. When you're ready to shop for back to school you will also come across the Halloween candy. While you're busy shopping for Halloween they've already put out the Christmas décor. By the time you get around to those last minute Christmas items they have already put in their order for Valentine's Day. The mistake many Etsy sellers make is being extremely short-sighted. You can't wait until a particular shopping season has arrived to begin to create or promote those associated listings.

Now maybe you're thinking well I just do my own thing and I don't get mixed up with a bunch of other niches or even the holidays. Too bad it doesn't make a difference. Whether you're selling cactus wall art or Swarovski wine bottle stoppers, the rest of the entire country is engaged in these various shopping seasons and holidays. If you're smart you will take full advantage. I would often try to jump on a bunch of bandwagon trends right before Christmas hoping I could see equal success as another seller. What I didn't realize is that the same seller had created their design and listing months prior. They already had a lead on catching the earlier shoppers so by the time the holiday rolled around, they were so far ahead in the algorithm and on the first page that it felt impossible to try and capture that same audience. We all know what it means to be the consumer but you have to put your seller hat on. Stop waiting until the last minute and get ahead of the competition. If you know every single year pumpkin spice flavor is a huge hit starting in September, why on earth are you waiting until September to start advertising your pumpkin spice candle you sell? 3 months early is a good rule of thumb to follow when you're preparing for an upcoming season or influx of interest.

 A great resource I have found to be really helpful is a niche calendar or simply just a holiday calendar. There are several online for sale or you can create your own. The calendar is a tool to assist you in planning out your year. Maybe your particular Etsy shop encounters the same type of demand during a particular quarter or month. If you can anticipate the needs of your customers in advance, be assured you will beat many other sellers to the punch. Go all out and even run a sale or feature those particular products higher up in your store. An extra tip is to make the product appear sparse. People are more likely to take action when you create urgency. As I began to incorporate more planning I no longer felt rushed to keep up with the different shopping seasons.

Etsy is a go to platform for gifts so any way you can make your products or services appear more gift oriented, the better. You also want to make sure you have your photography and mockups ready to go. If you wait until the middle of the season to decide all of a sudden you need a group of women advertising your product instead of just one because it's wedding season, the person who already has it posted will steal your potential customers. Also don't be afraid to make multiple listings for the same product. Bonus tip. Copy is one of the greatest features I have discovered on Etsy. You can copy an entire listing and only alter a few details while still creating an entirely new listing. You have to be careful if the listing is integrated with another system especially when it comes to the title however, it's a quick technique to get more of the market share in search results.

Perhaps you already have a great listing that has been working well however summer is approaching and you want to cater to shoppers who may be going on vacation soon. Long before summer approaches you could create a second listing using copy and target those customers. Tags are another great detail to modify. Even if you're using the same listing, you can always go in and change your *gift to her* tag to *mother's day gift* or whatever else you may foresee as being relevant in the near future.

If you're already running advertising, make sure your advertising is relevant to the season and the upcoming environment. If for example you're transitioning to summer then you may not want to be advertising a model wearing shorts in your promotion. Some of the best-selling products do so well on Etsy because the seller goes the extra mile. For example if they're selling nail polish in the month of march, they're going to advertise it with a model wearing green for St Patrick's Day or promote their shades of green more that month and months prior. It can seem like a burden making so many constant changes but it can also make all of the difference.

Etsy has a lot of competition so you want to catch the customer's eye. A trick I learned is to really help the potential customer see themselves using my product or if it's a gift, see their friend or family member using it. Be particular in how you promote your listings. Even when it comes to social media, if you have an audience of teenagers than use models in that age range to speak to your customer and post other content you feel they would be interested in. Perhaps you add a song that's popular with your target audience on top of your crafted, targeted promotion. If you're not confident you can create top notch photos yourself than find someone that can. Buy pre-made mockup images and simply add your design to it.

Remember, every effort you make is an investment. When you're walking around the mall, do you look in the store windows and see a mannequin just lounging around haphazardly with any old frock on? Absolutely not. Someone researched the trends, engaged with their customers, and styled each piece to perfection on paper alone long before you ever saw it displayed. Be intentional in how you present your Etsy shop. Have a reason for everything you do. If a specific banner or order of products are displayed in your shop, there should be a why. Make adjustments often and have a vision for every move you are making.

BAD MOCKUPS

I touched on this earlier but stop posting your listings any kind of way. Invest the money and purchase quality mockup photos. If you have the skill or know someone that can create the image you want first hand then go for it, but stop listing your products as if you were in a hurry. If you're running a print on demand business and the supplier is providing mockup photos then you have to ask yourself, is this really the best I can produce? How many other sellers do you think are also using those average, plain mockup photos? Add your flair, style, and branding to the image.

Think of your customer and what would attract them to buy. If you need more inspiration then visit a few big retailers that sell a similar product and take note of what they're doing. How's the lighting? Are they using models? Is the background all white or is it more of a lifestyle photo? Mockups can single handedly make or break a customer's decision to buy. Even if you're photographing the images yourself and not relying on a digitally crafted photo of your product, it doesn't mean the photo is competitive. If you can't compete with the digital mockup photos where you buy an image of an all-white mug for example and then add your design to the front of it in Canva or Illustrator, then you may want to rethink the look of your listings.

Real life sample products can provide a great advantage but they still need to look good. Offer the right lighting, provide related context when it comes to the background, and make the product the highlight of the photo. For a long time I had subpar listings and I won't lie, I still landed sales. But they don't compare to the sales I obtained when I stopped posting mediocre images and invested in quality. The mockup photos are the last area that you want to skimp out on. I couldn't imagine going to a restaurant and every single photo provided for the different entrees looked unappetizing and taken on some old Android. I don't think I would be brave enough to continue. Don't make your customers think too hard. You want to make their decision very easy. Show them why your product is the best and the time you're willing to invest in providing a sensational image. Multiple eye-catching images are a huge plus.

Be sure to try different options when it comes to displaying your products. I made the mistake of always showing just the product alone. Over time I noticed a better response to when there was a model present. I also explored being more inclusive and diverse. Don't be afraid to use a model that looks like the girl or guy next door. More than likely you will have all types of races from different backgrounds so be sure to think of them. The female population on Etsy is in fact the majority however there are a lot of female shoppers searching for gifts for the men in their lives. Test out a few men in your listings if applicable and see what the response is like.

Be considerate if your product is unisex. I had a lot of great selling products that appealed to both men and women. Well I took some bad advice and started catering only to my female audience. Instead of providing a more androgynous look that didn't really target either gender, I blatantly appealed to women. I lost a lot of sales from that mistake. Finally I realized my mistake and added back listings with my previous mockup style however I'm sure I lost customers to other Etsy shops that hadn't been so hasty to only target women. You really want to be mindful if you're operating in a particular niche or area that is prevalent with a specific race and be sensitive to your listing decisions. If I wanted to list a product that celebrates Black History Month then I'm going to opt for a black model. Again remember, the customer should be able to see themselves using your product. It's not to say only certain models can sell a specific product but the extra attention to detail can make a huge difference in a positive way.

Don't be tone deaf. Show your customers you do have some knowledge of what you're promoting and not that you just want a sale. Often you may see a lot of the same mockups and models all across Etsy. Do not be discouraged if you also are utilizing the same image. I guarantee many of the customers are not deterred by it and simply want to buy the most appealing product. I use to intentionally go out of my way to find model photos no one else was using or hide the face if it was a popular image but who really cares? Sometimes you have to take a more tunnel vision approach to your store and just do what's best for your business.

TAKE A BREAK

Building and maintaining an Etsy store especially when you have big goals really is a full time job. I know the hours can be long and at times you can feel as though your efforts aren't translating to sales, but whatever you do, just don't stop! Do not take your foot off the gas. Keep going. Keep pushing forward. Continue to create. Continue to brainstorm. There is always more work that you can do. Always improvements that can be made. There's more to learn each and every day. I made the mistake once of getting comfortable. I was seeing double digit sales numbers consistently every single day and I thought to myself, I have made it! This is fantastic. I'm just going to sit back and enjoy this.

But while I was sitting back taking a break, the next seller was learning, creating, and putting in the effort to surpass me. If you've been selling on Etsy long enough then you know that most trends and ideas don't truly belong to anyone. Sure there is a lot that is copyrighted and I wrote an entire chapter on trademark infringement. However more often than not, that popular phrase or style that seems to be selling like hotcakes can be replicated by anyone. Sure you may be the first to do it but you won't be the last. Someone else is looking to steal your success and not just do it like you but do it better than you. A lot of my best sellers at the time were copied for lower prices, with better mockups, and faster shipping. If you're sitting back just taking a break, how can you be improving and keeping your customers happy? Look at McDonalds. They didn't just rest after they created the dollar menu. Yes it was standout when it was first created but their competitors started to drop their prices and offer a competing product for a similar price. We know McDonalds has added to their menu and they've taken away. The restaurants don't look how they did 20 years ago or even 10 years ago. They're always reinventing themselves. Forever changing. They know how to change with the times but they also know what their bread and butter is. They have not lost their brand identity while they've done their best to stay number one.

    When is the last time you reviewed every listing in your store and tried to figure out what you could be doing better? Have your refreshed your mockups in even the last year or 6 months since you've been open? I have done a complete overhaul in relation to the look of my store once before and although it was time-consuming, well worth the effort. Find someone reputable that can review your Etsy shop and give you a few pointers for improvement. If you can find another store owner that has done extraordinarily well, that's a plus. I've had my shop critiqued twice and both times received valuable information to take my business to the next level.

    I respected the last reviewer so much I even changed my branding. I was so crazy about this one shade and after listening to her I went through all of my store, social media, and anything else that had my store information and altered the one color that was attached to my store. No regrets at all because it was not only on trend with the current color palette but overall just easier on the eyes. I previously used a really popular mockup site that had awesome graphics and a wide array of models doing every pose you could think of. After my last critique I noticed that the models were not wearing the exact replica of the product I was advertising and it was pretty obvious. I immediately took down any mockup that I thought could be misleading and went for a more realistic look of the product. That move saved me a lot of confused customers and bad reviews because the customer expects to receive what it is you are advertising. Be mindful of every small detail.

If you're listing a certain brand of sweatshirt for example and you're promoting your design on a sweatshirt with clearly a different brand that is misleading. I actually received that very complaint in the past because the customer zoomed in on the label and based off that image alone, ignoring all other details, she ordered an incorrect size because of her experience with the other brand shown. If you have a product that isn't selling, get a sale and if it is selling then make it a best seller. The listing image is what will catch the customer's eye first so be dedicated to continual improvement.

Have you learned anything since opening your Etsy store or even just reading this book that you plan to implement in a major way? Wherever your skillset may be, you should be getting better each and every year. Learning about the process, learning about your customer, and being prepared for your next direction. Before I even opened a shop on Etsy, I had already begun learning all about Adobe Illustrator. In my mind it was the number one software for design and at the very least I wanted to be able to create a few basic elements for my products. I am self-taught so I sought out many self-guided tutorials. Half the battle was just learning what every feature does and when to use it.

Trial and error has always been my best teacher so sometimes you have to jump right in and see what you can come up with. How much do you know about the full process of your products and the industry? I would receive questions from customers all of the time wanting to know more about the process and if I was using this technique or another. Initially I had no clue. I began to educate myself on the full process that I had outsourced and why one technique was superior to another. Otherwise I could be missing out on a much better method. I also began to learn about the materials used and what I personally preferred so that I knew what my customers were receiving. I'm not saying you need a sample of every product or service in your store but you should at least have a fair amount that you have physically held or reviewed so you're not completely in the dark regarding the customer's experience.

Etsy is also always changing so you have to keep abreast of what they're doing and learn how their changes can affect your business. There really is so much you can always be learning whether it's new trends, social media strategies, marketing tips, new product ideas, customer preferences, and the list just goes on and on. If you're not learning then you're not growing and you should want your Etsy shop to grow to number one. You can do it!

ABOUT THE AUTHOR

Keela Butler has spent the last several years exploring the ecommerce industry as a retailer and designer. She started out studying the retail space first hand in the local stores of her hometown Richmond, Virginia. Her specific interests centered on inventory management and visual merchandising. She later moved on to studying in the classroom. Keela is a graduate of Virginia Tech with a Bachelor's Degree in Merchandising Management and Liberty University with a Master's Degree in Business Administration. In this book Keela reveals the secret science behind selling on Etsy and the pitfalls many will face. Discover how ten major mistakes she has encountered can translate to your success. This book provides specific, actionable techniques every Etsy seller should know.

www.ingramcontent.com/pod-product-compliance
Lightning Source LLC
Chambersburg PA
CBHW050301220526
45465CB00002B/774